I0165307

steam rising
from a full bowl of rice

steam rising
from a full bowl of rice

ZEN MASTER
DŌGEN

VERSIONS

Stephen Berg

with an Afterword by Steve Antinoff

ZIG ZAG
PRESS

Copyright © 2013 Stephen Berg
Afterword © 2013 Steve Antinoff
All rights reserved

ISBN 978-0-9890912-0-6
Library of Congress Control Number: 2013904086

Composed in Palatino fonts
by P. M. Gordon Associates, Inc.

Published by ZIG ZAG PRESS LLC, Philadelphia, Pennsylvania
Distributed by MILLICHAP BOOKS LLC

For information, contact:
pmillichap@sbcglobal.net

To Dan Dietrich

Contents

II

III

IV

Author's Note

I am grateful to have used Steven Heine's fine scholarly translations of Dōgen's five-line poems as a basis for writing most of my versions. Heine's translations appear in his book *The Zen Poetry of Dōgen: Verses from the Mountain of Eternal Peace* (Tuttle, 1997; reprint, Dharma Communications, 2004).

—SB

I

ZAZEN

That idea
Moon mind water
It's enough to make me puke
Waves rush up freezing my bare
Bright feet

TRAPPED

White white clouds
And snow
And me pinned down
On Echizden between rocks
Blind in fog and snow

REFUSING WHAT DŌGEN SAYS IT IS

A halo
Framing the boat
Moonlight soaks the oars
Waves no-identity waves
And the rower

WHATEVER YOU DO

I guess we seem unreal
To ourselves
What a weird thing that scarecrow
Stuck into the paddy field
As useful as I am

THIS VERY MIND IS BUDDHA

Duck seagull
Bobbing between
Foamy crested
Waves that
Reach up

ON WORDS

Talk's easy is it possible
To say what says itself
Go ahead explain explain and explain
What says itself doesn't explain
No matter what you say

WAKE THE NOTHINGNESS MIND

Geese come and go
Like us
We barely exist Dōgen says
People never forget
The trail of the birds

AWAKE

It's like this
Just when I yearn
To see Kyoto more than ever
Sections of a field a flower a branch are so
Beautiful

WINTER

Fabulous those yellow leaves
skittering across my floor
All night
The dangerous mountains
Stern shrouded with snow

54 YEARS

Still alive!
What can stop me?
Still demolishing cursing heaven
Alive without the tiniest desire
Life death a white-hot iron wire

DŌGEN

Who me Dōgen?
The bitter end of spring
And I still want to be here
As if someone dies
When I die

WATCHING THE MOON

Stuffed with gruel and rice I let myself go
That cloud the muttering water
My shabby robe
Flapping like a fish
Donkey's head glides by

THE POINT OF ZAZEN

Deep water fish swim like fish
Colossal sky
Birds fly like birds
That's how it is
Don't want it don't try

INCONCEIVABLE MIND OF NIRVANA

True as usual
Cherry trees their resplendent
Fierce pink never changes
Leaving the house
Where I was born

ZAZEN

Moon
Right here inside
Me
Ablaze
With a trillion wavetips

NEAR DEATH

October
Maybe I'll see November
Meanwhile
Drenched in blue moonlight
I stay awake

II

This whole thing
About being a Buddha's pathetic
I'll paddle anyone across
On my raft built of
Twigs glued together with birdshit

How could I do
Anything but stroll down
"The path" strewn with
Dung where else
Could I walk?

Ride the four horses
Of anguish of what we still call
Concern kindness compassion the "true way"
It's enough to drive anyone insane
And ride the four horses

It kills me
The twilight cicada chanting
Its refrain
If that's what it is
The day's wiped out forever

So complicated words
Petals blown free
A kind of suicidal satori
In an unknown
Mind

WILDFLOWERS

The mildest breeze
Conducts their fragrance
Everywhere
Even the frozen peaks
Even the frozen sea

Alone on the road
My sadness wrapped in a linen sleeve
I babble pray
Kindness from the
Eternal source shields me

YOU

Winter is
Crackling thunder
Snow gusts lash the pines
Mist-hidden
What would you call it?

Even for the poor
Spring bursts
Through the gates time to pluck
Young herbs
Wade through the transient fields

Spring dusk
Blows off like sand
In a flash night
My endless treks
Taut as a bowstring

Inescapable cherry trees
Bloodstained leaves
Gone so soon amazing
If they could talk
If we could talk

Even asleep under my
Bamboo roof I pray
Every human being
Is saved then after I die
Those who are left

Without looking back to see my footprints
I tilt my head toward
A voice calling me home
Though everywhere
Is home

Only people who hammer themselves to the bone
Will find it but even if
Your house isn't blown down
Summer winds still rake the trees
Night a mask across my face

All my life wrangling with
Right and wrong I relax in moonlight
Yes the same old nostalgic moonlight
For years I brooded over the pristine
Immortal mountains

Easy to do
Nothing hour after hour
Untouched by time
Somewhere else
Call it "the way"

I have not known who I am
Terrified
By that then found out
Like the blue sky
I'm the dog with its everactive tongue

RAHAI

Worship that's what Dōgen still calls it
Here we go again—
White heron
Hiding in the snowy field
Of invisible grass

Greedy wren
Building its nest on its head
While a spider designs
A web of tiny crabs
Over its eyebrows

For a split second
No ears or sound
No words
No listener
Touch me

Summer begins
Slumped in my hut
Time to change robes
And one last thing
Burn my seedy bamboo screen

Mind isn't wood or stone
A thing you can see
What holds
Us here is
Like dew congealed to frost

Icicle
Dripping
From a
Mosquito net
Are you a Buddha?

Tip
Of an elephant's tail
Frozen in the window
Though nobody
Holds it back

Blade of grass
Studded with dew
Dawn breezes
Soothe my cheek
Awake or not

Plants
Don't have hearts like us
Yet they wither
My bones catch fire
Beholding this

Snow keeps blowing down
Into the steepest gorges
Sonata from who knows where
Confusing me
Up to my knees in flowers

Even to this stranger Dōgen
Roses pansies but also
Immaculate sky
Mind I offer you
Buddha's black rocks

Been here forever in this
Leafy shack
Cut off words
Are stones I can't use to speak
Peonies crowd my door

That gray disc
Skimming the peaks
Is not my friend
Ideas like ripped silk
Scurry across its face

III

INNATE REALITY

Insects whine then
Snow and all
Those avid fantasies
About shedding body and mind
Choke me

MOON

Considering you
It doesn't matter who I am
Swallowed by the pale shadows
Of your vacant
Call it beauty

OLD

I'm old
Some nameless creature moans
was was was was was
Maybe from a tree maybe in the sky
Maybe me

MIST

Weightless
As a grassblade
I seem to be floating
To Kyoto
In a mist dense as a thicket

NEVER IDLE

Does everyone feel
Permanent anguish
Caused by the streams
And luminous foliage
At dusk?

RAIN

Still cannot believe
Idiotic drops
From the eaves
Become
Me

CIRCULAR DELUSION

I used to believe
Beginning and end made a circle
Like tangled hair
When it's pulled out and straightened
No longer a dream

ME

A miracle my face
In the stream
Speeds by so fast
Nobody blur
I can only stare

ZAZEN

Ah moon
Finally Dōgen
Focused like a needle
Crumbling into
Splintered flame

MUJO

The crane shakes
Raindrops from its beak
Just to make it clear
Moonlight reflected in the drops
Means nothing

LITTLE LIGHTS

What I love most
About my childhood
Is the same thing Dōgen loves
Lightning bugs so faint they fade
Into twilight

IV

ALSO

When I wash my face
In the mirror
I want to leave
My hands
Over it

THEM

Isn't it true
Even your children die
Tell me
Is it possible
I mean really possible?

FACES

My parents had faces
Like mine didn't they
Once?
Now my face
Is my face

MY FINGER

Out there
I'm pointing to it
The tiniest star
Aches
Just like my heart

IN A DREAM

I came back
After I died
To see my friends
Eat drink talk exactly
As before exactly

ALONE

Sometimes I sit bolt upright
In the middle of the night
Afraid but of what
Of what
What?

OLD MAN

I put down my reading glasses
On the bedside table
I know I did
Right there
On the table

SAD

Nearly about to leave
This world
My consciousness
Snuffed out
In one eye blink

THIS

What you think you did that was kind
And therefore memorable is not
Nobody will remember you or it
Yet being here to say this
Makes what I say a lie

Ember in the Ash

IN THE LATE SPRING AND SUMMER of a recent year, I visited poet Stephen Berg more than 20 times in three different hospitals. At first he slept through most of the visits, sometimes the entire visit. Twice as I was leaving he opened his eyes and asked where I was going, yet as soon as I sat down fell asleep again. After surgery he was in an artificially induced coma for three weeks, wrapped in Velcro to prevent movement. He emerged from this bedraggled, legs thin as arms without much clarity, almost lifeless, a tracheotomy tube down his throat. He could not speak but pointed to things in the room in ways that I did not understand. He signaled for a writing pad and wrote messages that I sometimes, with great effort, could figure out. Whenever it was time to depart, he signaled me to come toward him, and squeezed my fingers with astonishing force.

When Kuei-shan insisted to Pai-chang that the brazier contained nothing but dead ash, Pai-chang stirred the ashes, uncovered a small ember, and said to Daigui: "What do you call this?" One day the ember, from his hospital bed, pointed to an item on the hospital bureau. I lifted several objects that lay on the surface. Each was rejected with a wave of a finger. Finally I held up a heavy, hard-covered tome of American blues lyrics someone had brought by. I brought it to the bedside as beckoned. It took the patient several minutes to get his hand to write what turned out to be an inscription. More finger gestures let me know the book was a gift to me. It read, with some bits scribbled out: "For Steve, & Steve finally is dead now. Steve."

The well-known *waka* of 17th-century Zen Master Shido Bunan runs:

> While alive be a dead man
> Thoroughly dead,
> Then, do as you will,
> All will be well.

Pai-chang demanded exactly this by showing Kuei-shan the ember in the ash; Dōgen asserts it through his famous: "Body and mind fallen away; the fallen away body and mind." That "Body and mind fallen away" is not a state of meditative concentration but what Zen calls the Great Death is a point often made by the great Zen master Shin'ichi Hisamatsu:

> The totality of bodily modes of being (*nikutai no arikata*)—sitting, standing, lying—and the totality of mental modes of being—feeling, will, thinking; in short: the totality of the actions of man will not do (*ikenai*). Nothing other

than this is spelled out in my fundamental koan: "Nothing goes? What do you do?" Herein lie death and resurrection. True sitting (*za*) is neither sitting of the body nor sitting of the mind, but *shinjindatusraku* (body and mind fallen away): body and mind die together and are reborn.

When Stephen Berg finally returned home from his hospitals, I called on him. I could not believe the speed with which he scurried about like a cockroach with the light turned on. When one of his daughters pleaded with him to use his walker, he barked: "Claire, go to hell!" Too irascible for Hades, Berg was back.

〰

BACK FROM WHERE, exactly? Stephen Berg surely is not a "dead man living" in the Zen sense. In all the years I have known him he has been skeptical of Enlightenment even for the Zen masters who claim it. Yet he can't keep away from the Zen personalities who *do* claim it. That contradiction is the driving force of these "versions." The Enlightened Dōgen we have come to anticipate, ecstatic and calm, sensitive to cosmic beauty, is steadily undermined by a curmudgeon Dōgen, blind, angry, pinned—either unable to awaken or, more troubling, awakened to an awakening that is of no significance and changes nothing. Berg's Dōgen pukes at zazen and rejects body and mind fallen away as a fantasy. His many ecstasies are a hell of a lot of fun, but they alter the human condition not a whit.

"Back from where?" is answered, for me, in the poems of Part IV. Toward the end of Part III, Dōgen, too, is fallen away:

Finally Dōgen
Focused like a needle
Crumbling into
Splintered flame

This is not simply Dōgen expressing the great death; it is Dōgen left behind, for he is in the way. Part IV is Berg as alone as any human can be. The nine poems he includes there are those of a man on loan from death, written in an ink mix of death and last breaths. Leaves on the verge of dropping from their stems—though Berg, cranky at the cosmos with his intense grip, will likely stay dangling from the branch hung over the precipice another hundred years.

Steve Antinoff

www.ingramcontent.com/pod-product-compliance
Lightning Source LLC
Chambersburg PA
CBHW032048040426
42449CB00007B/1035